Advanced Praise for
eat salt | gaze at the ocean

Moving through language and lineage, past a
political, *eat salt | gaze at the ocean* is an info
work from a bold and exciting voice unafraid
Désil addresses the reader with grit, remindi
readers this is our history, too. Referring to the hundreds of Black
people killed by law enforcement in 2016 alone, she probes, "you might
almost want to say *this list is not Canada* – i dare you." "come in recede
further come in again," the poet beckons us into our still-present pasts.
"how to write about what you carry but don't know?" This ambitious
debut presents a powerful answer to that question.

—**Natasha Sanders-Kay,** *SubTerrain Magazine*

In her engulfing debut collection, Junie Désil offers poems that
recalibrate my heartbeat. She engages in a fathoming of the inherited-
ongoing personal and social – holding each and holding each
accountable: "i write this Black body live / i wish for the kinds of lungs
that breathe in salt-heavy hostile seas." Through language and forms
and imagery that abscond and astound, there is a scope and current in
this work that does nothing less than overturn (in the sense of the root
of catastrophe) the litany itself.

can we talk about the ocean in the room?
the elephants have left

secrets submerged in brine salt scouring wounds

I say this out loud, within earshot of the coast and without fear of
reproach: the ocean will never be the same.

—**Hari Alluri**, author of *The Flayed City*
and *The Promise of Rust*

eat salt |
gaze at the ocean

poems

Junie Désil

talonbooks

Talonbooks
9259 Shaughnessy Street, Vancouver, British Columbia, Canada V6P 6R4
talonbooks.com

Talonbooks is located on xʷməθkʷəy̓əm, Sḵwx̱wú7mesh, and səl̓ilwətaʔɬ Lands.

First printing: 2020

Typeset in Minion
Printed and bound in Canada on 100% post-consumer recycled paper

Interior and cover design by Typesmith
Front cover artwork by Cecily MacGregor-Gauntts

Talonbooks acknowledges the financial support of the Canada Council for the Arts, the Government of Canada through the Canada Book Fund, and the Province of British Columbia through the British Columbia Arts Council and the Book Publishing Tax Credit.

Library and Archives Canada Cataloguing in Publication

Title: eat salt | gaze at the ocean : poems / Junie Désil.
Other title: eat salt / gaze at the ocean
Portion of title: gaze at the ocean
Names: Désil, Junie, author.
Description: Includes bibliographical references.
Identifiers: Canadiana 20200202847 | ISBN 9781772012651 (softcover)
Subjects: LCGFT: Poetry.
Classification: LCC PS8607.E85 E28 2020 | DDC C813/.6—dc23

for Nadia, with love. always

Being haunted draws us affectively, sometimes against our will and always a bit magically ...
—AVERY F. GORDON
Ghostly Matters: Haunting and the Sociological Imagination (1997)

how do I live free in this black body?
—TA-NEHISI COATES
Between the World and Me (2015)

I

origins | beginnings | of sorts

here.

it's not the same ocean i know   but ocean is
ocean and it's salty   you still have to watery-squint

your eyes when the sun blazing scorches the surface
shimmers   the horizon shifts   it's still the same sound
pattern of the recede

come in recede further come in again   the sound of pressure
builds crashes pounds
the tug and insistent pull when you're in tune with the
ocean   sink toes this land
borrowed far from another   this constant
familiar uneasiness

how to write about what you carry but don't know?
strange inheritance   one carries
everyday code   understandable if borne of Haitian soil

submerged in salt sea   bracing rivers   falls

i start with origins
i was not here   i am not there

rather

the line from here   today tethers collective trauma   umbilical
centuries old

those bones a bridge over oceans
triangulated   passages

abridge | / əˈbɹɪd͡ʒ /

and so:

succumb
      let go

(i'm afraid)
       i'll be overcome

envahie
     engulfed
          swallowed

  instead
      stoic

 i keep this ocean
           behind   my eyes
                  my heart

at bay
slow   grab drag rake

sudden emptiness of the
ocean floor

rationalize   trace the origins   collective trauma
here   scattered   there
no real home   (as in) what does it

                              matter   it's
                              happened

zombies reimagined response

                    enslavement

                    etched in bones

ask mother
about zombies   *the back-home kind*

she won't speak except to start.   and stop.
words caught in her throat

i ask Father
I am a man of God. Don't pay attention to such things.

silence.

so i ask books from the library   keep them from
touching other books

or caressed by the same night wind against my back

i ask for help   guidance to write these words.   offer a prayer
remembering:
give thanks   before asking favours. zombie
zombification process

dezombification

Haitian zombie   ask the library and the internet vague and also
specific questions (at least eleven different ways)
i used " " * < >

i tried zombie – walking dead   even   comparative
                                   (vs.)

salt   ocean   eat salt   *réanimation*

at night the pile of library books   stay
outside my bedroom
René Depestre's *Hadriana in All My Dreams*

Wade Davis's *Passage of Darkness* maybe the books   with *vèvè*

drawings like stick and poke tattoos their shapes arrows
                          draw   down

            the *loas*
        to language of gods i don't know

i don't want supernatural gifts
jump at shadows   words rattle about stop their noise
as SkyTrain wheels
screeeeeeeeeeeeeeeeeeeeeeeeeeeeeeeeeeeeeeeeeeeeeeeeeeeeeeeeeeeeeeee
                          around the bend
luminous eye of the train blind my wide-open
ones

wonder if i've accidentally summoned these gods to wake this husk
crack-of-the-whip call
(our dead's lips sewed   black thread or wire   might not answer)

stuck.

i ask for help
   read accounts appropriated
reinvented white tales of zombies   watch

i am legend   28 days world war z
night of the living dead   shaun of the dead
izombie   warm bodies
walking dead   santa clarita diet
dawn of the dead

now mass-culture   mass-consumption zombie
disease vector technology symbol for
                  mindless labour
                  (not quite slave labour)
                  everyone for themselves zombie
                  sexual liberation taboo

zombie-futurism
                  in which zombie
                  has   consumed the consumerist escapist
                  fantasy

when Mother   disappears into the crisp
winter darkness

to:
re-member old (white) folks
zombie-like shuffle (Alzheimer's/Parkinson's)
fend off unwanted advances
(*he's old he doesn't mean anything*)

while Father   sits   blue Mercury idling   breath   fog
wait – they'll rummage in her bag to make sure
no thing has been lifted   theft

against company policy.
simultaneously ply her with stale bland Christmas-cake charity
(*also, against company policy*)

triple shift: work nights during the day cook and clean (no pay)
between snatches

sleep

petrified   i've absorbed   fear

                    somewhere

                    lullabies and kisses
                    stern admonishment
                    on my deportment
                    (How to Be a Good Black Girl)

                    between

            harried cooking instructions

curious   anxious questions shooed away or responded to

don't remember

         child-sleep   late-night crawl on my
           belly snake-like

listen to

       adult conversations   hushed-toned over back-home food

heavy buttery

       yellow Haitian cake   chased down with instant coffee
       lait Carnation

or sweet

       thick jewel-red   green vodka syrup   or *crémasse*
                        creamy smooth

               (guests only)

strain
to hear the Haitian patois
voices rise

          fall   punctuated

    preternatural lullaby

                          silence

                        between

                        fickle

                    remembrance

                      memory

how to write about zombies:

                          when you're a generation

removed from the soil

                                       and

several generations removed from   *lan Guinée*

                                       and

colonial words   crowd your mouth
still your tongue

                                       and

sever the connections
between   land   language   self

                      whitewash at best

how to write about these things that terrify

                                     and

                  resolve into odd shapes at night

                                     and

lurk
      in shadows
                  of the smooth heart muscle

joints of bones' marrow   tip

                          of fingers
and

                          tongue

how to talk about zombies without resorting to magical thinking (say white people) but to understand zombies you have to understand God (believe it or not) and to understand God you have to have faith and to have faith you have to understand God a tautological loop no doubt more magical thinking and some serious syncretism my presence on these occupied territories is also syncretic but it hasn't seeped into my bones or the cartilage that cushions and pads

just bone on bone
weary grating questions

this is how to write about zombies

-
-
-
-
-

silence (met with silence)
dread imbued in every cell
feverish search

write about zombies   you'll need iron will

brace your heart

the suitcase in the closet: *ne touche pas*

passport pictures landed immigrant cards   school assignments
spidery colonial handwriting marked by nuns
priests   a notebook   filled with handwritten Haitian recipes (!) among
the mementos

sepia-toned *National Enquirer*–esque newspaper

                    headline screams *zombi!*
                         (think bat boy)

left side of the page

advert in *créole* for Haitian peanut butter (fiery smooth *mamba*)

(i was seven maybe eight)

if i haven't misremembered   a man slack-jawed   blank face
bug-eyed
nearly white

ombres/z'omb'e (français) shadows jumbie juppy/duppy
(West Indian languages) ghost zemis (Taíno) souls of the dead
zumbi (Remosam/Bonda)   by way of Portuguese slave traders
ndzumbi (Ghetsogho) cadaver

zombie (American English)   consumed en masse

zom·bie | / 'zɑmbi /

1 a:

there are worse things than ghosts
worse than spirits that make you cry   laugh incessantly
(it doesn't matter)

worse things than hauntings
than spirits crouched in corners
nursing ancestral wounds

ancient family magic   on both sides   collide
suck life   will
I'm losing weight   she says

teeth are falling out   lisps
asthma   wheezes
breath catches   weeps   spiderwebbed glass heart

she will die slowly but she won't really die
(that's important)
she will be pronounced dead (that's very important)

the guardian of the cemetery
summons   she zombielike

b:

on a visit to Haiti 1991:
at the airport, Father is stopped by a woman. she tells him he is dirty,
his clothes ragged – would he like a bath? he's been too long from home
he *forgets*. in fact he is not dirty, his clothes are not ragged
it's just code for *ou gin movè zespri.*
he carries many bad spirits; a bush bath is in order.
he says no.

on a skype call 2017:
Father tells tales, jokes. repeats them twice, starts another one,
interrupts himself
let me give you a joke my girl.
his nephew while they skyped together
exclaimed: Uncle! your face! alive–no longer like a zombie.

2 a:

faces blue-glowed
unwavering   our pursuit toward   more numbness
feel   but not too much
don't   look up
wear   human-cancelling headphones resolutely
earplugged
          hearts too

don't feel [because] we can't feel [ourselves]
hearts   eyes
dulled   do/what/we're/told/to so we do

what we're told

b:

gait   a shuffle he   in shambles
eyes wide and blank
(is that drool?) down-turned
smile

touch him   no one else seems to   fingers   connect
gingerly
surreptitious wipe of
hands on   thighs
tentative   damp   two-cheek kisses   between
his adult siblings

when he brings bolts of cloth (cradled in filthy off-white
corner-store bags)
for Mother to sew   into dresses   they sit months on end on
the closet floor
no explanation   just angry hisses   hand gestures   don't ask

Mother won't tell   we know to not hug him or receive his gifts
he talks   spittle flies from his mouth   stopper our ears
mimic   blank stare

our hearts   mine
break   watch   through corner of eyes
trapped   mind empty

c:

Mother newly single
she weeps incessantly   i think her cowardly
at times for her unwavering faith   how she looks
forward to this shiny heaven
believes herself   ruined and yet accommodates

accommodate.

we have made accommodations
Guinea is heaven and heaven Guinea

there is
beauty in believing in an after so hard
                    a balm for the present
wounds

ground-up bone
small tree frog
polychaete [segmented] worm
large New World toad
pufferfish (tetrodotoxin)*

exhume.
then:

administer
jimson weed (*Datura stramonium*)
(*q.d., b.i.d., t.i.d., q.i.d., continually as needed*)†

---

* in small amounts: euphoria, numbness, and tingling
   in sublethal amounts: heart rate non-existent, conscious/aware
     but unable to speak, breathing imperceptible
   in lethal amounts: death

† psychoactive compound: disorientation, delirium

Code pénal, article 246, paragraphes 2 et 3

[Est aussi qualifié attentat à la vie d'une personne, par empoisonnement, l'emploi qui sera fait contre elle de substances qui, sans donner la mort, auront produit un état léthargique plus ou moins prolongé, de quelque manière que ces substances aient été employées et quelles qu'en aient été la suite.

Si, par suite de cet état léthargique, la personne a été inhumée, l'attentat sera qualifié assassinat.]

in ~~other~~ English ~~words~~:

this   attempted murder
making of a substance that produces lethargy but not death if buried in that state of lethargy after ingesting said substance   attempted murder irrespective of the outcome

II

transatlantic | zombie | passages

gon·zo | / ˈɡɑnzoʊ /

1:

Seabrook journalist of sorts writes *Magic Island* (introduces and
popularizes the zombie)
      his accounts neither "fiction or embroidery"
            gonzo

before Hunter coined the term (1971) just embedded journalism
(coined 2003)
      American military personnel stationed in Haiti (1919–1934)
land publishing contracts

write about their exploits. before gonzo   embedded military before
embedded journalists
      reporting subjective   history repeats itself   repackaged

nothing new   just the same (narrative thread). lightheaded   either
the Dunhills or the thread
      likely both

smoke ring into the light-studded sky   white zombies
play on
      play on
         play on

      phone screen

The Pennsylvania Gazette

NEWS FROM THE WEST INDIES

—Boston, April 19, 1792

Since our last, several vessels have arrived from Port-au-Prince, all of which bring the most gloomy accounts of the situation of that island; the distresses of which appear to be owing, not more to the revolt and devastation of the slaves, than to the enmity prevailing among the freemen, and the want of subordination to any government.

About the 13th of March, the negroes attacked the town of Leogane – set fire to the plantations on the plain, and were joined by the negroes thereon, who had till then been in quiet servitude: after much fighting and burning, the negroes retreated. Many were killed on both sides – the lowest number, including all parties and colours, is stated at 1,000.

Capt. Wellman, of Salem, who sailed from Port-au-Prince the 23d of March, at evening, informs, that 1,000 militia and 500 regulars marched out that morning, said to be on account of the insurrection of the negroes on several plantations on the plain, who had drove their masters into town. – That they were met and opposed by the mulattoes, whose head quarters were only 4 miles from the town. – That he saw numbers of wounded brought into town while he was on shore – That the battle continued all day – and that its issue was unknown when he sailed.

A detachment of the regular troops had been called for, by the municipality, to go to Leogane, at the time of the negroes attacking that place, and boats were prepared to transport them; but the officers refused to embark – as they said their orders were to defend the town of Port-au-Prince – they therefore could not answer for their quitting their station. For the same reason, they had also refused to march to the plains around Port-au-Prince. But the clamours of the populace, and of the private soldiers, being for action, the municipality caused the officers to be arrested, and sent to the Cape, in order to be carried to France. After this, new officers being substituted, the troops marched out, as before mentioned.

The effects are to be dreaded, whatever apparent pleasure the event may give to many descriptions of people.

[the seismic fault line runs through the island of Hispaniola.
    the fault lies in the people of Hispaniola]

televangelist Pat Robertson:

And, you know, Kristi, something happened a long time ago in Haiti, and people might not want

to talk about it. They were under the heel of the French. You know, Napoleon III and whatever.

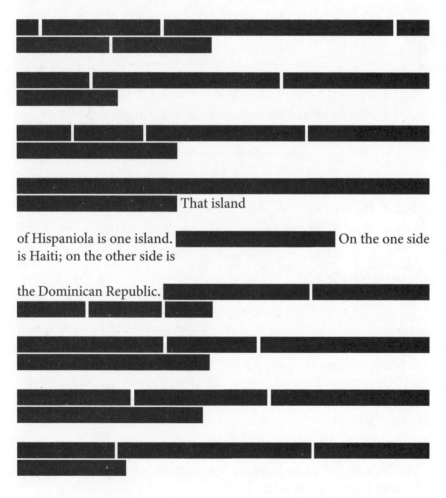

That island

of Hispaniola is one island. On the one side is Haiti; on the other side is

the Dominican Republic.

A

PARTICULAR ACCOUNT

OF THE

INSURRECTION

OF THE

NEGROES of St. DOMINGO,

Begun in AUGUST, 1791:

TRANSLATED FROM THE FRENCH.

The FOURTH EDITION:

With Notes and an Appendix extracted from authentic
original Papers.

1792.

*SPEECH made to the NATIONAL ASSEMBLY,
the third of November, 1791, by the* Deputies *from
the* General Assembly *of the French Part of*
St. Domingo.

[...] The incendiary was a negro-driver* of Desgrieux's plantation. Armed with a cutlass, he fled; M. Chabaud saw, pursued, and overtook, him; they fought; the negro was wounded, taken, and put in irons.

Being interrogated, he deposed, "that all the drivers, coachmen, domestics, and confidential negroes, of the neighbouring plantations and adjacent districts, had formed a plot to set fire to the plantations and to murder all the whites."

---

* The French word is *commandeur*, signifying a negro trusted with the care of a small party when at work.

live-wire warmth
dead giveaway give way   give away

emptiness walk alongside me
unseen tread heavy

weight of history press
follow out of breath   struggle

heart is a muscle   untrained to
lift carry attend to these wounds

in the company of the undead *ghostly matters*
deal with the ghastly

(forgive) the repetitious   a long-winded account
we tell stories twice
sometimes more   different angles
so you *feel* the story

[January 12, 2010.
magnitude 7.0 – aftershocks – 52 registers
after.   shock.]

white church spire   toppled
point heavenward

damned accusation   surrounded
by coloured rubble – colonial pinks

pastels   white sugar dust
coated

bodies,   hills
pile like blankets

broken wails broken hymns

broken prayer   like the white
church spire toppled point

heavenward above   the hope
these broken bodies

piled like blankets   the land
too broken   too scarred

to cradle   a last embrace
families on knees
send prayers

upward   the sun   what God
hastens the breaking of

skin, tissues, cells, ligaments
overwhelming streets, morgues

mass graves   coloured rubble
colonial pinks pastels and white

sugar   dust-coated prayers, broken hymns,
broken bodies, church spire pointing

sins and parents

here's a story about dead men working sugar fields.

worked for the Haitian American Sugar Company (HASCO)
HASCO founded by Charles Steinheim, John Christie, and Franck Corpay.
August 5, 1912   registered in Wilmington, Delaware, with a five-million-
dollar capital

1915 HASCO's operations under "threat"
anxieties over German business interests
need to dominate and secure economic interests in Haiti
U.S. marine invasion and occupation.

1918 HASCO increased need and demand
bodies to work the fields
more bodies

bonuses on wages as incentive
entire families register their bodies
more bodies
to harvest sugar cane

old man, Ti Joseph
his wife Croyance
bring bodies
more
bodies
harvest   bitter
sugar

anyway.
those dead folks working the sugar-cane fields like it's 1820.
about that.
Croyance felt sorry for them. all that work in the fields for HASCO
          bland food.

took them to the market. it would be fun   she thought.
had already fed them
          unsalted boiled plantain
          and meat.
          bland food.

they were zombies after all.
                    single file   shuffled to the market.

spied a vendor selling *tablette* – sweet peanut brittle
this would be nice
          a treat.

they ate the *tablette*. salted.

reanimated
leapt up   ran off toward their respective graves.
reburying themselves.

free.
                    to finally die.

another story, this one on origins.

Africans being "precious cargo" but dispensable.
to prevent them jumping off ship to their deaths
were told a story of not reaching Guinea
home   promised land

heaven.
punishment eternal mindless
toil   the curse   zombie.

like current conditions
                    that hell is fresh.

still.   heaven.
homeward-bound
mother's celestial cane keeps her
          balanced holds her upright
the promise of "gold-paved streets" twelve
gates to this shining city

reward for not-living
suffering earth

risk eternal bondage for freedom now
live free or die
in the end

life.
your body fights you to stay
alive it wants to   stay
alive   you don't want to

i know

my right palm   coloured sweet-sticky cerulean blue from
        the pills   masquerade as tic tacs fill
mouth round   click
        against my teeth the surprise   bitter
                powder melting inside
cheeks   i fought   life

stay   awake alive drool piss   at fifteen
i ~~should have~~ had ~~so much potential~~
~~and~~ reason

[we left the island because it was broken;
everything was broken. we were broken]

your hands dry earth
network of criss-crossed spidery blood rivers
too numb to have them scratch tenderly
my wet-reared face

smooth catch   soothes the night terrors
carry over in the day
wrinkles leather ridges you worry-scratch
the side of your index finger whisper

hum a day lullaby post night shift
the cracks widen like bloody fjords
you dip from amber-brown glass
doctor prescribed unctuous steroid

makes your skin strong
tough as hide protective gloves for
when you clean bodies   wasted tenderness
surrogate to Alzheimered physicians

don't recognize loved ones
they sure help you remember your station
check your bag
clear plastic that smelled like my pink jellies

the bag you bought at Eaton's bargain basement
didn't stop white wrinkled shaky hands from rummaging
just making sure. there's a dear!

Attachment:
a fancy word tossed around in therapy
for care reserved   meted out equally between affluent clients
while we simultaneously push   pull   strain   love

a fancy word
for your polished precious stone worries
rolled between your fingers   prayer bead-like
preoccupied

they convince you that bringing a child into this world cut out of your womb severs bonds that might have been had baby been pulled out of canal that the hardness between Mother and i is the result   what if i tell you the hardness grows comes to be alongside your growing in the womb in preparation for our encounter in the world our womb water wet black bodies have already been in peril   imperiled a thousand lifetimes ago a thousand lifetimes ahead the hardness that is glassy-smooth shield an heirloom forced on us what if i tell you that preparation is a five-hundred-plus-year tradition the thing about hard exteriors   i want to tell you about shells   they're hard for protection i want to tell you that nothing gets through that exterior

(except sometimes those very same undead folks   the one who watched in fear out of the layers of tissue fat grist – her first i was pulled she drug-zombied remembers nine months preceding it all comes down to knife slide baby out bloody and tiny on a noon Sunday she'll say she never laid first eyes – on her breast i was placed – everything throbbing the next day baby heavy already burden)

nothing gets through that exterior except that trauma-bonded love you know – hard i want to tell you another thing about hard exteriors how they form black bodies amber-like stone absorb fossilized – hard but not diamond-hard still   it is up to us to shine diamond-bright to be the worth when the climate   the weather dictates otherwise

> are we even human beings or just
> incarcerated bodies and dead flesh
> —ANDRAY DOMISE

i want to tell you what it's like to be born unloved already despised by this world   born carceral mother's womb cell narrow passageway reproduced brick i want to tell you what it's like to be born of specters   DOA spells *B-L-A-C-K* and still these fleshy ghosts birth me i want to tell you that the primal sea rocked me the womb a ship's hold reproduced in wood and iron shackles – there is no pastness

another story.

along the countryside up north deep in the bushes up in the mountains
inaccessible the lay of the land unfamiliar to the 330 marines
insurgents hide in these places irregular forays   offensive attacks
none of them wear uniforms
or coordinated ones at that   their weapons similarly uncoordinated
stolen
from the previous century:

antiquities
swords
sabres
bayonets

hoped-for wishes that these last imbued with the victory of the first
successful (and only) Black revolution red swathes of scrounged red-
cloth armbands the only unifying symbol
the recruits are hauled out of:

beds
yards
villages
towns
wrested too young
too old from mothers'
    breasts
regardless and the choice limited:

    a) corvées or
    b) Cacos –

    a) chain gangs build infrastructure or
    b) insurgents

launch out of landscape familiar as the back of their hands

Black Jesus | Charlemagne Péralte | 1919
the old door unhinged doubles as a cross   no nails rope wound
around his torso   under armpits
hold lifeless   body

two bullet holes
from a .45
through
the heart
handsome head
lolling
left
loin cloth
barely covering
flaunted by
American personnel
intended to tamp down
the rage
burning

Cacos' checkpoints
red patch on arms
black as night the only markers delineating who they are
two American personnel faces darkened with black cork
pass by
pass as black
Charlemagne Péralte
(never camping in the same place twice and surrounded by armed guards)
betrayed by Black Judas
one of his own generals
passing as Caco
black face   shadows blending
pass checkpoints
two bullets .45
through the streets
Charlemagne's body crucified
only fans
        incendiary resistance

in the countryside   sparks brighten the wind
the black-and-white photos brandishing his body
ignite further insurrection

how to make a zombie-nation

salivate on the potential and continued wealth of Haiti
greedily eye the strategic location and importance of the island
panic about German interest in Haiti
panic some more over German control of international commerce
(80 percent)
panic even more about the impact of unrest on American business
interests (HASCO)
acquire control of the Haitian government's treasury
take Haiti's gold reserve and
transfer to Federal Reserve Bank of New York
panic at anti-American revolts by Haitians
invoke the Monroe Doctrine
invade the island with U.S. marines (1915)
designate 40 percent of Haiti's national income to repaying debts
install American-backed presidents
dissolve the legislature
rewrite and impose a new constitution (overseen by Roosevelt)
allow foreigners to purchase land
(illegal since Haiti's independence – 1804)
ratify a treaty
granting the U.S. economic control of Haiti for ten years
enable veto power
to American representatives over all decisions in Haiti
establish the marines as administrators
impose conscription and forced labour
press censorship
increase violence and sexual assaults by marines
establish a "disengagement agreement":
withdraw after nineteen years and four months (1934)

act as debt collector for France

to be this valuable / this hated
—JUNE JORDAN

this is the paradox

in the ocean where we were disposed of by drowning or shark ravaging
salt-brined unmarked graves paradoxically our freedom the very molecules
of sea-womb water we are here we still remain our DNA ingested and
upcycled by every single organism our bodies extracted ingested this
probably made your heart lurch and sink and beat and flutter all at once
if i say that in fact time is unable to absolve/dissolve if i say five hundred
years ago we were bondaged bodies if i say that despite the passage of time
if i say that time in this case is measured in *residence time* and that five
hundred years is not five hundred years ago that past horror is not past
that it is *present time* if i say our ancestors are still here we are still here
if i say that we are zombies we are ghosts we are traces we are *revenants*

this is what it means to defend the dead: a long (tragic) love poem to
our undead
selves

Tu viens du Passage

to answer where are you
　　　　　from i must tell you i come from the ocean

i come from the middle passage
　　　　　　in between one home

and another　　wrested forcibly placed on ships insured
　　　　　　ensure black bodies

worth (less) cargo not quite worthwhile
　　　　　　a triangulated passage

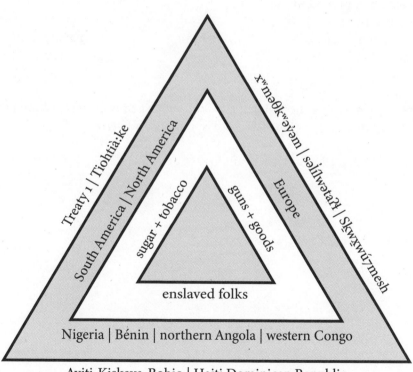

listen.

this is not a poor us
it is exhausting to write about slavery, ongoing oppression
as if that's my only history or point of interest   origin
in fact it is *your* history an interruption
your attempts on our life
trauma porn
as if i don't want to write about other things   banal musings

here.

we are a haunting the haunted a spectre a ghost a revenant or a zombie
this is how you remember us as we re-member ourselves

    we are here we keep coming

my childhood bombarded with black-and-white images of "the poorest nation in the western hemisphere" i learn this bit of history from my parents long after they tell me to lie about where we are from or bend the truth a little *say we're from France – remind them that you were born in Montréal* long before i came to know it as the place *broken in two* Tiohtià:ke long before i learn that the "pearl of the Antilles" the mountainous island we're from is Ayiti-Kiskeya-Bohio.

this is what i learn – that on the eve of the new year, dissatisfied with his secretary's initial draft of the Haitian Declaration of Independence, Boisrond-Tonnerre says, *nah, the statement does not capture what we revolutionaries have been through; it does not get to the heart of* La liberté ou la mort! – *Live Free or Die.*

We require in fact for our declaration of independence:
the skin of a white man for parchment
his skull for an inkwell
his blood for ink
and a bayonet for a pen

General Dessalines: *chef's kiss* *i entrust you to convey my sentiments regarding the above*

III

eat salt | gaze at the ocean

can we talk about the ocean in the room?
the elephants have left

secrets submerged in brine salt scouring wounds
flayed open flesh history

sharks bloodhungry devour bodies
       self-projected or thrown

later you'll fear the lack of sovereignty bestowed upon me
     – a *birthwrong*

it is what will make your corded forearm tighten   grip   fear that
lifts and falls your anxiety on young flesh

i'll harm-protect you first before the
       world inevitably does

the ocean like the Lord and the Devil   gives and takes away its
memory
          long   drags as it scrapes the seabed

recedes, pulled by moon   salty grief and hopes
          secrets left behind treasure-like

black-torpedoed hurtle, sink *free at last*
          you've had dreams

fears. your wildest imagination cannot conjure the worst of
          reality. you're not prepared for your future

children *born Black that's dead on arrival*   you forget to check
          fat wrists and ankles for the imprint of shackles

forget to run your palms smooth over the salt-scabbed welts their
          new bodies   carry

ring clank of iron chains keys to bars
          ocean remembers   reminds the little ocean in the womb

breaks spilling life-water and   death to come

this is what the ocean did: lured   with true promises of freedom even
        when there was no choice

"bury me in the ocean with my ancestors 'cause they knew death
        was better than bondage"

these are the number of bodies at the bottom of the ocean:
        there are no accurate numbers

we've swum in our ancestors' blood   salt-warmed vermillion bath

after so many years the bones are bleached sand the ocean
        liquid sandpaper
those that have been documented properly = two   five hundred
to a thousand
wrecked   five found

sometimes you'll find a part of a ship in an estuary that tells the
story of a
        wager or a boast. Captain Foster "born in Nova Scotia of
English parents"

"... slipped away from Mobile as secretly as possible so as not to
arouse
        the curiosity of the Government"

here is the thing about water   its very nature contains but does not hold
    secrets
Captain Foster reached Mobile on Sunday morning in August 1859; his
    return from the slave coast having been made in seventy days

– the Clotilda *scuttled and fired ... placed seven cords of light wood*
upon her

        after discharging the last of 116 or so Africans
        long after slavery was outlawed punishable by law   death even

the point of all this scudding back and forth through history   the
thing
          about secrets in water   *a piece of lumber with square*
nails in it

ghost ship from the 1850s   they may not stay submerged

     we still need to talk about the ocean

the secret of the last slaver sunk and burned in Alabama's bay
        resurfaces in 2018 and *Barracoon*   unpublishable sees

light of day   dear Alice Walker, thank you for breathing
        Zora Neale Hurston back from relative obscurity

dear Zora, know what my mama would say? that you poked your nose in
        business you didn't understand   you wrote:

*I am breaking a promise by writing this, and maybe the cocks are crowing
        because of it …*   Ma would say you knew the hour of your death

ba moun "give man" there is always something   for something and Zora
        you gave me an account not perfect but not littered with

        nigger lazy stupid beast dumb childlike

i would pull out my best Black Girl China for you my elder just to hear
        your accounts of the day-to-day of Haitian life

your hat dapper stylishly tipped   jaunty angle – imagine if i told Ma that
        you were in my living room enjoying Haitian sweets and drinks

talking about zombies   her heart would seize in terror her hand would
        grab mine and like all those who warned you:

        there are many good things for you to learn and *perhaps it will
        cost you more than you are willing to pay*

it's certainly not the ocean's fault

it is traditional to destroy the Black body – *it is heritage*
—TA-NEHISI COATES

I can't breathe

words gasped in death
  breathe life into Black Lives
matter i have searched looked at the names
those who have died at the hands of this direct line
from and descendants of slave owners
  from and descendants of the system
    descended of a system that violently captured and
  enslaved Black people
      law enforcement
       law *enforcement*

this system, its heritage the destruction of Black bodies

and so:

this poem you are reading took me three years to write. if we're counting and being accurate, it took me over twenty years to write. i took a snapshot of 2016. i counted. over two hundred deaths in one year. if we're being comprehensive, this right here does not include the dead from the transatlantic slave voyage, those who leapt to their deaths, who died beneath the cargo hold, once stolen from their ancestral lands. those who died in violent capitalist servitude, who died in violent encounters with white holders of enslaved **Black** people, this list does not include those who died scattered about the various colonialist projects and expansions on stolen lands. this list does not include those lynched. this list does not include those incarcerated in the ongoing carceral projects – a direct line from the institution of slavery. this list does not include those who have died from any of the leading causes of death among **Black** people, who are the result of continued structural and systemic racism underpinned by violent and ongoing land theft and dispossession of **Indigenous** Peoples. this list contains recognizable names of people who died in 2016. this list also contains names unrecognizable to me or to you. this list does not contain the names of **Black** folks further marginalized even in their deaths – **Black** trans folks. *they will need another page.* this list does not include sex workers preyed upon and discarded – *they too will need another page.* this list does not contain the ones disappeared and forgotten by most. this list is a year of headlines darkened by these deaths. sometimes the headlines are bold and loud and other times tiny columns after a deep rabbit-hole search – "*see more*" or "*related stories.*" this list is a list of names of **Black** people who have died south of this "border," so you might almost want to say *this list is not Canada* – i dare you. this list is an *i dare you* to tell me that this is not about race, that this is not anti-**Black**, that this is not purposeful. this is a piece that will go on for a while till you feel as paralyzed as i continue to be. till you feel your heart leap out and flop wetly, thud dully outside its protective cage. this is 2016. only a year, a snapshot of names that may or may not have gone viral, that may or may not have been distributed with "*trigger warning*," "*content warning*." this list contains the names of **Black** people who had faces, who had stories, who had aspirations and hopes and even if they didn't, we had hopes and aspirations *for them.* this list does not tell you of their dreams, their joy and pain, their struggle. this list of names had pictures attached to these names. sepia-toned, grainy, black-and-white pictures of young men tatted up, white-tanked, with babies in their arms. this is a list of boys under nineteen, under eighteen, under seventeen, under sixteen, under fifteen, under fourteen, *just thirteen.* this is a list (albeit smaller) of women, young women under nineteen, under seventeen, under sixteen, under fifteen, *just thirteen.* with children, holding their babies, selfied, dazzling smiles aimed at the camera. this is a list of older folks, sixty-one (!), seventy-two (!), who should have lived to see two generations of data (DNA) transfer. this list contains the names of folks murdered by the states' handlers, by law enforcement originating in the violent need to protect stolen land for land holders, their forebearers, catchers of enslaved folks, their legacy assured. this piece will keep going till you feel almost numb, almost as numb as i feel, till all the names *bleed together into unrecognizable inky blood.* till you, in an exercise in futility, attempt to memorize these names. i will have read these names over and over and over and over till: survivors' guilt. till you mute posts/people on facebook because *not today.* this list does not include all the names of the **Black** people whose deaths inspired riots, inspired movements for us by us. this list should make your guts twist on themselves. should make you feel horror. should make you wonder what fresh hell we live in – what horror story is this. this list that you can't see but surely can search should make you weep, in shame, in anger. this list should make you double over in pain, this list should make you feel each bullet hole, each taser shock, each chokehold, violent pavement slam, black boot(s), fists, palms. this list should make you *curl fetal.* this list does not include (of course) those who survived, who survive, who put one foot in front of the other. this list of names does not offer contextual information. this list does not tell you that every day i roll a kernel of fear rosary-bead-like between my fingers, praying that those i love do not end up on this list. this list does not tell you that there've been close encounters and that my fears are well founded.

this list is 2016. a snapshot of those killed.
by gunshot
by taser
by death while in custody
by vehicular strike
by unknown
by other
by violent encounter with law enforcement

i don't name them   how
could i make space in this heart-mausoleum in case
practise saying the names closest to me   recall them
i want to ask if you ever worry if your heart squeezes and holds till the
next day
relaxes only fitfully   at night   anxiety follows
disrupted circadian rhythm

(for a made-up identity)

Father's never met a cop who doesn't respond to respect
#NotAllCops he tells me:
>   *i was walking by two cops in a rough part of Toronto*

there were young Black men with nothing to do their pants down low i
walked by and
>   *said hello and they nodded*

in a Facebook post to a well-known Black activist: *you must have been*
doing something
>   *they don't just stop you for walking while Black in a park*
>   *anyway, smoking in parks is illegal in Vancouver*

my father's been detained by police because a neighbour called
fearing for his mental state
>   but #NotAllCops   yet Black and mental health and and
>   and just Black = death by cop

a college professor stopped on his way to work because he "fit the
>   description"
>   5′11″, 160 lb., puffy jacket and a knit cap   grateful for the *sister*

>   in the red coat she watched while he was being detained

i too am grateful for the friend who stopped with me at the corner
>   of Commercial and Broadway
>   he Indigenous, i Black – the intersection where cops police
>   Indigenous and Black youth

stopped with me to witness a Black man being arrested he stopped and
witnessed
>   cops swarm   crowd parts, eddy around the obstruction

stopped and asked if i wanted to go closer   asked if i wanted to witness
>   if i wanted to stop and feel my heart squeeze   blood

my mouth dry   limbs helpless my mind racing   wondering: *is he?*
did he? shame
          coursing cold face hot   did i want to witness regardless of what
he did

or didn't do   witness being Black at the hand of cops   did i want to
take responsibility
          for this man face ground down into icy pavement neck at an
unnatural angle

back weighted   black boots   judge   drown deep in respectability i
don't ask
          is he okay?

what i need to ask is if i'm the kind that would leap cars and part bodies
plant feet
          in front   shout down the cops and crowds

                         lift up our right to be

my feet rooted in place says i'm the kind who might as well tut-tut
silently
          move along

i let you down
                    forgive me
                              forgive me
                                        forgive me

there are too many names to commit to memory
others nameless or given names not their own
these blur and sink into each cell
leaden
absorbing anti-Black
dead now   i've made a mausoleum
of this visceral fat   cradles tendons supported by bones
i've ingested communion-style
dried salty tears wafer-like on my tongue
mute prayers lullabies to send them past
that liminal watery grave space

residence time

i witness black crowns askew too heavy
slip
aslant past their eyebrows
            pants that shorten their stride to a tired shuffle
zombielike

here as
intermediary between no home un-home what's home
and ocean-cradled souls

i write this Black body live
i wish for the kinds of lungs that breathe in salt-heavy hostile seas
life to live in an ocean of Black love a warm bath

if i gaze at the ocean
can i undo the zombie curse
no longer be *"proximate to death"*

i look at the ocean
it breathes loudly
i stare at the ocean and wonder
when will i feel alive

SOURCES

P. vii (quote)
Gordon, Avery F. *Ghostly Matters: Haunting and the Sociological Imagination*. Minneapolis, MN: University of Minnesota Press, 1997.

Pp. vii and 68 (quotes)
Coates, Ta-Nehisi. *Between the World and Me*. New York: Spiegel & Grau, 2015.

P. 28 (quote)
Code pénal [1835], art. 246, para. 2–3. In Tribunal de cassation (Haiti) and Linstant Pradine. *Les codes haïtiens annotés: Contenant 1° La conférence des articles entre eux, 2° Sous chaque article les titres des lois et actes tant anciens que nouveaux qui les expliquent, les complètent, les modifient, les arrêts du tribunal de cassation, 3° Une table générale des matières, 4° Une table chronologique des arrêts; Code d'instruction criminelle et Code pénal*. Vol. 3. Paris: A. Durand et Pédone-Lauriel, Éditeurs, 1883. Retrieved February 25, 2020, from Google Books. books.google.ca/books?id=gPgrAQAAMAAJ.

P. 31 (quote)
Seabrook, William. *Asylum*. New York: Harcourt, Brace and Company, 1935.

P. 32 (newspaper article)
"News from the West Indies." *The Pennsylvania Gazette* (Boston, MA), May 2, 1792. Posted by JD Thomas on Accessible Archives, "News from the Haitian Revolution" (blog entry), July 14, 2016. www.accessible-archives.com/2016/07/news-from-the-haitian-revolution/.

P. 33 (excerpt from an interview transcription)
James, Frank. "Pat Robertson Blames Haitian Devil Pact for Earthquake." *National Public Radio*, January 13, 2010. Accessed February 25, 2020. www.npr.org/sections/thetwo-way/2010/01/pat_robertson_blames_haitian_d.html. Video interview on YouTube: "Pat Robertson Blames Haiti Earthquake on 'Pact with the Devil,'" interview by Kristi Watts, January 13, 2010, www.youtu.be/S5nraknWoes.

P. 34 (quote)
Saint-Domingue, Assemblée générale, Commissaires Jean-Baptiste Millet and Samuel Elam, with the French Assemblée nationale législative and West India Planters and Merchants (London, England). *A Particular Account of the Insurrection of the Negroes of St. Domingo, Begun in August: Translated from the French; Speech Made to the National Assembly, the Third of November, 1791, by the Deputies from the General Assembly of the French Part of St. Domingo.* London, UK [?]: s.n., 1792. 1–2. Retrieved February 25, 2020, from Internet Archive. archive.org /details/particularaccoun77230sain/page/1/mode/2up.

P. 39 (reference)
Seabrook, William. *The Magic Island.* Illustrated with drawings by Alexander King and photographs by the author. New York: Literary Guild of America, 1929. 95–96. Retrieved February 25, 2020, from Internet Archive. archive.org/details /magicislandbywbsooseab.

P. 46 (quote)
Domise, Andray (@andraydomise). "Are we even human beings or just incarcerated bodies and dead flesh?" Twitter, February 3, 2020, 12:32 p.m. twitter.com/andraydomise /status/1224430394763829249.

P. 50 (quote)
Jordan, June. "The Difficult Miracle of Black Poetry in America." In *Some of Us Did Not Die: New and Selected Essays.* New York: Basic Civitas Books, 2002.

P. 63 (quote)
Coogler, Ryan, dir. *Black Panther.* Burbank, CA: Marvel Studios, 2018. 134 min.

Pp. 64 and 65 (quotes)
Hurston, Zora Neale. *Barracoon: The Story of the Last "Black Cargo."* Edited by Deborah G. Plant. New York: Amistad (HarperCollins Publishers), 2018.

P. 67 (quote)
Hurston, Zora Neale. *Tell My Horse: Voodoo and Life in Haiti and Jamaica.* New York: HarperCollins Publishers, 2009 [1938].

Pp. 75 and 78 (quotes)
Sharpe, Christina. *In the Wake: On Blackness and Being.* Durham, NC: Duke University Press, 2016.

PERMISSIONS

Portions of *eat salt | gaze at the ocean* appeared in slightly modified forms in the following publications: *The Capilano Review* 3.39 (Fall 2019), guest ed. Juliane Okot Bitek, 12–19; *G U E S T: A Journal of Guest Editors* (chapbook), issue 10 (May 2020), ed. Jenny Penberthy, unpaginated; and *emerge 17: The Writer's Studio Anthology* (Creative Writing Program at SFU Continuing Studies and SFU Publications, 2017), 203–204. Thanks to the editors.

ACKNOWLEDGMENTS

Gratitude to the most high. And apologies if I miss anyone: it is not intentional.

To the revolutionary foremothers – your names are rarely acknowledged, though you fought in front, behind, and alongside for the liberation of Ayiti: Sanité Bélair, Marie-Jeanne Lamartinière, Empress Marie-Claire Heureuse Félicité Bonheur Dessalines, Henriette Saint-Marc, Suzanne Simon Baptiste Louverture, and many more courageous women.

To the Black women writers, some of whom I came to late, who have been an inspiration: Toni Morrison, Audre Lorde, June Jordan, Nikki Giovanni, Dionne Brand, Christina Sharpe, and Edwidge Danticat – the very first Haitian writer I read. Her book *Breath, Eyes, Memory* (1994) set the course for me believing I had something to say.

When I first moved to Coast Salish Territories, I was young (nineteen). At the University of British Columbia, where I was a student, unused to a thirty-two-thousand-plus student body, isolated, and one of few Black students, I struggled. A classmate in my African American history class, noticing my struggle (sobbing openly in class, etc.), facilitated a connection with Dr. Yvonne Brown. I am grateful for that introduction; it quite literally saved my life. Dr. Brown was instrumental in keeping me in class, hiring me as a research assistant, and sparked what is now my mode of looking and examining and following the "colonial trace" of seemingly mundane objects. While I have not pursued what I thought would be a career in academia, Dr. Brown reinstilled in me a love of research and learning. I am ever so grateful.

To the folks of Colour Connected Against Racism UBC – the OG crew, thank you: Gurpreet Singh Johal, Kyra Pretzer, Dara Akpan, Dionne Woodward, Bereket Al-Azar, Kobe Asiedu, Mwalu Peeters, Soleman Hashmi, Che, and countless other members who came through the years. You were the other part of the equation that kept me sane. Thank you especially for publishing my poem on *Ubyssey*'s (possibly inaugural) "Race Is the Issue"; y'all started what looks to be a lifelong passion for writing angry and impassioned poetry. Also the parties, the sleepovers, the trips, the protests (APEC, WTO, and everything in between), Bumbershoot, concerts, movie nights – dope dope y'all.

To my roomies and forever friends Cherlyn McKay (original agent and first reader) and Kyra – when we realized the racist-roomie situations we were all in had to end. Thank you for creating a home for nearly a decade where we could let our hair down, breathe, be, laugh, and cry. To Mon Jef and Mwalu Peeters, Rob "MTL/Butler" Baxter for letting us have the Princess Towers and enduring *Love Jones* and us hollering all the lines all the time – "God is a Woman, OKAAAYYYY." We really should have bought the movie.

Wayde Compton – mentor extraordinaire to quite possibly every Black writer in BC. Thank you for taking a risk, for telling me *You're a writer*, for asking me to send you pieces. For the work and legacy of Hogan's Alley; those couple of years working on the project were also instrumental in my growth and understanding of the Black community here in BC. Thank you!

To the many Black women writers and creatives in this place – thank you for the work you do, for keeping it moving in spite/despite.

I am grateful for my time at SFU's Writer's Studio. Thank you Betsy Warland for your mentorship and kindness. Thank you Jónína Kirton and Zoë Dagneault for your mentorship, feedback, and friendship. To the Pigeon Poets (!) thank you for those nine months of sharing critiquing. Special thank you to Christine Leviczky Riek: thank you for opening up your home for multiple retreat opportunities – you are the consummate host.

Gratitude especially to Fatima Amarshi and Natasha Sanders-Kay for the organizing of writing retreats – a large portion of this manuscript was written during our time together. I am eagerly awaiting your forthcoming works.

Thank you gp for your friendship, encouragement, our intellectual conversations, our shared love of music and brilliant essays. And for the use of your apartment.

Thank you Naomi Moyer for your friendship and excitement over my accomplishments; I love that we're doing what we're called for and what we love. I love you. To Sarah Hedar, thank you; our friendship came as a welcome and delightful surprise. I am grateful for the hours of hangs, and commiserating, of work dates, and your general "Let's keep it guilt-free" approach to our friendship.

To Jen Currin for your friendship – so glad we met at Vipassana. Thank you for your heart, your generosity, and for reading through this manuscript. Your feedback was invaluable. To Shazia Hafiz Ramji, for your ongoing commitment to amplifying emerging writers, your sweet heart – thank you for your feedback on portions of this manuscript.

Julianne Okot Bitek – I have arrived (I think) and I thank you for being part of the welcoming committee :), your gently insistent encouragement, your beautiful curatorial talent in gathering poets – thank you. I look forward to travelling in the same circles.

To the Gatheration – the CREW. My beating hearts: Cecily Nicholson, Mercedes Eng, Hari Alluri. Honestly, you've all kept me going with pep talks, manuscript review, tough love, advice, amplifying, all while laughing, commiserating, and poeting (yup, it's a word!) together. I would not be here sweatin' over acknowledgments were it not for your support and care. I love you all. Thank you Thank you Thank you.

To my family: Manijeh Ghaffari for being the best mom ever – for spoiling me while I retreated at the farm, Jim Leuba for getting the cabin warm and toasty for my retreat, Anahita Sebti and Sara Sebti, my sistars – thank you for your joy and excitement at this accomplishment. Thank you for your love and care. I love you with all my heart – thank you for holding space for me while I disappeared to write.

Thank you Nushik – you are a wonderfully nice friend, and thank you for the use of your space to write. Madji the best cat ever – thank you for letting me squish-love you and for keeping me company as I wrote late through countless nights. I love you both.

To my love, my best friend, my rock, my party planner, my hype man Reza Sebti: this.man.has.not.read.one.page.of.this.manuscript. But he can gather a crew of people to show up at my readings. I love you, Reza. Thank you for your infinite patience and your support. Thank you for being so gracious when I abandoned you for weeks at a time to write in peace and solitude.

To the team and volunteers at Talonbooks: I have no adequate words to express my gratitude for giving this collection a home. Thank you to editor Catriona Strang for her edits and suggestions. To Charles Simard for such a kind and thoughtful copy edit, and in particular for the deep dive into some of the interesting bits I weaved in. Many thanks to Leslie Smith for the design work on this book, and for kindly incorporating my asks. And thank you to Kevin Williams for his assistance in the final cover selection.

JUNIE DÉSIL is of Haitian ancestry. Born of immigrant parents on the Traditional Territories of the Kanien'kehá:ka on the island known as Tiohtià:ke (Montréal), raised in Treaty 1 Territory (Winnipeg). Junie has performed at various literary events and festivals. Her work has appeared in *Room Magazine*, *PRISM International*, *The Capilano Review*, and *CV2*. A recovering academic, a UBC alumnus, and most recently a participant in Simon Fraser University's Writer's Studio, Junie currently works in Vancouver's Downtown Eastside, on the unceded and Ancestral Lands of the xʷməθkʷəy̓əm, Sḵwx̱wú7mesh, and səl̓ílwətaʔɬ (Musqueam, Squamish, and Tsleil-Waututh) and lives on qiqéyt (Qayqayt) Territory (New Westminster), juggling writing and life.